To PAULA
God has something wonderful
for you. You are not going
to believe it when
you see it. But
it is. Amen
Johnny
Roy

God's Name Brand

Clothing America and the World for His Kingdom

by

Johnny Ray Franklin

Bloomington, IN

Milton Keynes, UK

AuthorHouse™
1663 Liberty Drive, Suite 200
Bloomington, IN 47403
www.authorhouse.com
Phone: 1-800-839-8640

AuthorHouse™ UK Ltd.
500 Avebury Boulevard
Central Milton Keynes, MK9 2BE
www.authorhouse.co.uk
Phone: 08001974150

First published by AuthorHouse 1/4/2007

ISBN: 978-1-4259-4274-8 (sc)

*Unless otherwise noted, all Scripture references are
from the **King James Version** of the Holy Bible.*

*Printed in the United States of America
Bloomington, Indiana*

This book is printed on acid-free paper.

Foreword

By Leslie A. Green

When you ask a Christian what their purpose in life is, or what their ultimate goal is, they will tell you something along the lines of that it is to live a life that is pleasing to Christ, to go to church, read the Bible, be good to others, and ultimately, go to heaven.

If we look deep within ourselves to take a hard look at how we are indeed living as Christians, will we find that God is truly pleased? Or, in the end, will we be one of those that God turns away and says, "Depart from me, I know you not." Can you say that without a shadow of a doubt, 110%, you are going to have a place in heaven alongside the Creator? What can we do to secure a place in heaven? Even long after we become Christians and say, "Yes, Jesus, I do accept you as my Lord and Savior," we should never become comfortable with just having the title of "Christian." Are you still as hungry and curious as you were in the beginning of your walk with Christ? Many mature Christians and even pastors can lose their zest to be Christ-pleasing

Christians. Don't you have questions about the end of time here on earth? Do you wonder about the Trinity, and who Jesus, God, and the Holy Ghost are? Do you wonder about today's pastors, church members, and the church as a whole?

Are you required to speak in tongues? What is that anyway? Have you been baptized of water and Spirit? And what does being righteous or having faith really mean?

Christianity is not just a title and should be so much a part of you that people see Christ in you. However, if you do not regularly do the things that Christ would do and are not consistently seeking more knowledge as to how to be more like Him, how will you make it to heaven? Do you believe that all you have to do is say, "I am a Christian?" My friends, if that is your thought process you are in for an extremely rude awakening. You must believe that the devil is still busy trying to deceive us and keep us away from what has been promised by God. That is Heaven! We know that the only way to get there is through Jesus Christ our Lord and Savior. But it does take some work on our part to follow the Shepherd. Otherwise, we are and will continue to be lost sheep. God has laid out a plan for us and the plan is written in His holy word, the Bible. It has been the same for many, many years and will not ever change. It is up to us to follow His plan if our goal undeniably is to please God and make it to heaven. If you have questions, read His word to have them answered. Trust me, you will not be the only Christian to have questions about Christianity.

Many of us have the same questions and thoughts. This book shares some of those questions and answers. It is my prayer that the answers provided in this book by Pastor Franklin, through God's word, will open your eyes as they did mine. I pray that you never stop having a desire to completely please God and that you always have an everlasting thirst to make it to heaven.

By the way, I'm wearing my fine Brand-Name Clothes right now. Are you?

Table of Contents

Introduction

Greetings in the name of the Lord Jesus,

I thank the Lord God for this opportunity to answer questions on topics I believe are on the minds of Christians across the nation. The perilous times in which we live indicate that God is soon to come; therefore, the Lord has given us a charge to teach and preach the word to every creature. There must also be a knitting of hearts of all denominational leaders throughout our nation in obedience and submission to God's will and purpose. I don't know about you, but there have been times in prayer when questions came to my mind that I didn't know the answers to. I believe God incited these questions that I might seek after Him for the answers, and you know something, it worked. Through many years of prayer and fasting, God has illuminated my understanding of His purpose for coming down through forty-two generations. I call these revelations GOLDEN NUGGETS. The information contained in this book is very important to every believer. I believe that every aspect of life should be given some thought.

For instance, the world in which you live requires that you put on some type of clothing before entering it or just going outside. God established clothing for a covering because Adam sinned and knew he was naked. Now, if we are the offspring of Adam and knowing that we were "shapen in iniquity; and in sin did my mother conceive me," shouldn't we have some type of covering that we ought to receive on earth from God. Think for a moment, Adam's sin was committed on earth, not heaven. If God clothed him on earth, shouldn't God clothe us also?

My beloved brethren, this is my prayer: "Lord, open our ears that we might hear what thus saith the Lord and send a REFRESHING to America reviving our hearts with love for one another." I believe God has given White Raiment Ministries a word for the end time. This word will allow you to buy from God what you need for the preparation of His return. "I counsel thee to buy of me gold tried in fire, that thou mayest be rich; and white raiment, that thou mayest be clothed, and that the shame of thy nakedness do not appear and anoint thine eyes with eyesalve, that thou mayest see" (*Revelation 3:18*).

My ambition is to enrich every denomination with the revelation of God's purpose for the church. I pray that every minister would share this understanding in sermons with their congregations. God wants to use every believer for the work of the ministry. On your job, you can ask your coworkers, "Are your garments clean?" At the family reunion, you can ask your family members, "Have they purchased their wedding garments from Jesus yet?" In the marketplace, as you are looking and shopping for groceries, you can ask a fellow shopper, "What is God looking for in you?" They will ask you the question, "What do you mean?" Then your coworkers, family members, and fellow shoppers will proceed to look at you in amazement, because most of them have never heard or been asked such questions before. This will be your opportunity to glorify the Lord. Your answers are found in this book. I believe this ministry will usher in the presence of God's coming in the clouds of heaven, because that which the Lord is looking for, He will find on earth through your obedience to His Great Commission. May God bless you all. Amen.

These are some of the questions that the Holy Spirit has asked me over the years and have been answered by God through the Word.

1. Is Jesus' name the same as His blood?
2. God has a cure for AIDS and the HIV virus written in His word. Where?
3. What are the greater works that Jesus speaks of in St. John 14:12? If it wasn't healing or working of miracles, then what is the one thing Jesus could not perform when He walked on the earth?
4. Jesus said you must be born again. So how is a person born again of water and Spirit according to scripture?

5. What happens to a believer who is born of water but not of spirit, or born of Spirit and not of water? Where are they found in scripture?

6. If I, through faith, receive the blood of Jesus that removes my sins, how is the blood applied without a High Priest, if Jesus is in heaven?

7. Can I receive from God the things I need by faith without being saved?

8. Who is, or what is the Holy Ghost? Is He the third person of the Trinity? What does the scripture say?

9. The Bible says we will wear white robes in heaven. Are we wearing them now while we are on the earth or will we receive it once we get to the new heaven?

10. What is God looking for on Earth before He returns? Is it only faith?

11. Is there any place in scripture, which indicates that God requires you to speak in other tongues as a sign of having the Holy Ghost?

12. Did anyone in the Bible pray a sinner's prayer for salvation? Why do we pray sinner's prayers?

CHAPTER 1

Unity

David, the king, a man after God's own heart, writes, "Behold, how good and how pleasant it is for brethren to dwell together in unity" (Psalms 133:1).

And Paul, a man who once persecuted the church said, "With all lowliness and meekness, with longsuffering, forbearing one another in love; endeavoring to keep the unity of the Spirit in the bond of peace."

Therefore, we as a people that believe in the Lord Jesus Christ must come together in unity, speaking the same things in love, knowing that God lives in us all, through His Spirit. So let us take heed to what the Spirit is saying to the church.

The answers that we will share with you are answers given to us by God through revelation. For over twenty years, we have walked very closely with the Lord. And I thank the Lord for His friendship, His patience, His love, and His compassion allowing me to come boldly into His presence. I have a passion for prayer. Prayer is my safety blanket. Consequently, pastors have a hard time getting their members out for prayer. God revealed something to me that I think will motivate the saints to pray more. I'm a person that loves to look good spiritually and naturally. Whenever you pray, you are before the Lord. The word of God says, "Let us therefore come boldly unto the throne of grace, that we may obtain mercy, and find grace to help in time of need." Because of time, gravity causes our flesh to sag, and wrinkles with gray hair appear because of age. When you come unto the throne of God, you are in His presence, and God dwells in eternity. Notice, there is no time in eternity, and therefore, you are preserved in Christ Jesus. The more you pray, the younger looking you stay. Whenever you are in God's presence, the aging process slows down or may even stop while you are praying. Amen.

Is Jesus' name the same as His blood?

God has an unusual way of revealing his purpose in scripture. First, you must study to show thyself approved unto God. Secondly, His secret is with the righteous. Thirdly, there must be a hunger and thirst for righteousness. Every saint of God possessing these attributes will grow. Then pray for spiritual wisdom and revelation in the knowledge of Him (Ephesians 1:17).

Now, what is so peculiar about God is that He will allow you to read a scripture for many years and not understand its true meaning until He wants you to see it. This scripture, for instance, is a very familiar scripture that millions have read, but did they hear the voice of revelation?

"Then Peter said unto them, Repent and be baptized every one of you in the name of Jesus Christ for the remission of sins, and ye shall receive the gift of the Holy Ghost" (Acts 2:38).

Notice the name of Jesus is used for the remission of sins. Remission translates from the Greek word *aphesis*, which means forgiveness. Here we find Jesus' name being used with the same authority as His blood, having the power to eradicate sin. Hebrews 9:22b says, "…And without the shedding of blood is no remission."

Let's look at Acts 22:16 which says, "And now why tarriest thou? Arise, and be baptized, and wash away their sins, calling on the name of the Lord." Can a name wash away sin? Only if it's the name of Jesus Christ. The name of Jesus works with the same authority to cleanse (as His blood) and deliver whosoever shall call upon it. In this verse of scripture, Jesus' name is used as his blood.

Also refer to Acts 4:12 which says, "Neither is there salvation in any other: for there is none other name under heaven given among men, whereby we must be saved." In this scripture, we see that salvation is in the name of Jesus. Salvation means saved from destruction and the only thing that can save us from our sin is the

3

blood of Jesus. Here again, God's word tells us that His Son's name has the same effect as the blood.

So can we say that Jesus' name is the same as His blood? Yes, according to scripture we can do so theoretically.

The Bible tells us to call His name and upon calling His name, He shall save us from our sins. *(See St. Matthew 1:21.)*

God Has A Cure for AIDS and the HIV virus written in His word. Where?

God saved me in 1980. And a few years later, the demon of AIDS was known in every household across this nation, and fear gripped the hearts of the people as it did in the days of Goliath of Gath, that is found in second Samuel 17:4-11.

As it was in those days, God sent a savior whose name was David to fight for the people. We also have a savior for our day, the Lord of Glory (Jesus Christ). Amen.

I'm writing this to assure you that God has sent a word of deliverance for every AIDS and HIV victim.

In 1986, while reading the word of God, this scripture was magnified and lifted up from the page. The Lord spake to my heart and said,

"For I will cleanse their blood that I have not cleansed: for the Lord dwelleth in Zion" *(Joel 3:21).*

And I understood clearly what He meant. The question is how is this done? Simple, God will cleanse your blood with His own blood through regeneration. If you can understand Joel 3:21, you can understand how God applies His blood to all believers. This application is made through water baptism in His name. How can this be? Let's examine the word. When Jesus rose from the dead, he gave His disciples one commandment, and that commandment was to baptize all nations in His name. Why? Because when He walked in His human body as the Christ, His blood wasn't given or shed for sin. So Jesus had to wait until He was crucified and raised from the dead by the spirit of the father before He could do what He came down through forty-two generations to do.

I will share more with you about this topic in chapter three.

Please understand that once Jesus (as being the High Priest) has applied His blood unto you, there will be a noticeable difference in your physical body, which is received by faith, in reference to your healing.

Whenever you mention AIDS, homosexuality comes to the minds of individuals. But there are thousand of heterosexuals and children that have this disease also. People with this disease are feared by some church leaders. There is also great fear in the church of victims who have this disease. What are the fears? Some fear that the association of homosexuals with the young people will convey the wrong influence and some fear catching the disease.

The homosexual lifestyle is totally unacceptable in the true church, but the person should be loved and given an opportunity to be saved from this abomination. After being saved, there should be a period of time allowing the individual to prove that he or she has embraced the doctrine of Christ and has completely forsaken the homosexual lifestyle. God came to save those that are sick. Homosexuality is sin and a great sickness that needs the love and healing power of Jesus Christ, which should be manifested through His people.

Also, there are millions of people in Africa afflicted with this dreadful disease that must hear this word of faith. Is there anything too hard for God? I believe that if every person in Africa or wherever in the world who has AIDS or HIV would allow Jesus to wash them in His name (blood) through water baptism, He would cleanse their blood through His blood. These are not works on your part, but this is the work of Jesus Christ, for He dwelleth in Zion.

There are other scriptures associated with the blood of Jesus and physical healing. Look at Hebrews 9:11-14. In verse thirteen, it says, "For if the blood of bulls and of goats, and the ashes of an heifer sprinkling the unclean, sanctifieth to the purifying of the flesh…"

The purifying of the flesh is physical healing that is done through the blood of Jesus. This is clarified in the very next verse saying, "How much more shall the blood of Christ, who through the eternal spirit offered Himself without spot to God, purge your conscience from dead works to serve the living God."

Not only does the blood of Jesus cleanse your blood, but it also creates an awareness of sin according to scripture. When you have the blood on you, you can not walk around naked on the beach, knowing that men and women are lusting after your flesh.

"So then faith cometh by hearing, and hearing by the word of God." The blood helps you to live Holy. Amen.

CHAPTER 2

What are the greater works that Jesus speaks of in St. John 14:12? If it wasn't healings or the working of miracles, then what is the one thing Jesus couldn't perform when He walked on the face of the earth?

"Verily, verily, I say unto you, He that believeth on me, the works that I do shall He do also; and greater works than these shall he do; because I go unto my Father" (St. John 14:12).

This is a word from the Lord to all His people, that we might understand His purpose, and operation of the indwelling spirit.

Let us start with the grace of God. "For by grace are ye saved through faith; and that not of yourselves; it is the grace of God: not of works, lest any man should boast" (Ephesians 2:8, 9).

God's grace is undeserving on our part. "But God commendeth His love toward us, in that while we were yet sinners, Christ died for us" (*Romans 5:8*).

Surely, we can see that God has done everything for us.

1. He chose us in Him before the foundation of the world…. (Ephesians 1:4)
2. He called us….(Romans 9:24)
3. He washed us in His own blood…..(Revelations 1:5)
4. He filled us with His Spirit….1 (Thessalonians 4:8)
5. He keeps us that He might present us faultless…. (Jude 24)

Now, what is required of us? All we have to do is believe in His name and be obedient to the leading of His Spirit.

Now, we are coming to the greater works that Jesus spoke of. **The one thing Jesus did not do when He walked on the face of the earth as the Lamb of God is wash one person in His blood.**

Why? Because God sent Jesus as a Lamb to die for the world, and the lamb in scripture is not the applicator of its own blood, but the sacrifice. So, in order for Him to do His Father's will, Jesus could only function as a lamb while He walked on the earth. He could not wash anyone in his blood as it says in Revelation 1:5b, "unto him that loved us, and washed us from our sins in His own blood." The only thing Jesus could do as the Christ (God's fleshly form on earth) is shed his blood as the Lamb of God. In order for Jesus to function as the applicator or sprinkler of blood as the High Priest, He had to die and be glorified by His father, then come back as an eternal High Priest in the form of the Spirit, so that His priesthood might be an everlasting one. Now, this everlasting Priesthood is after the order of Melchisedec, King of Salem. (See Heb.73-7.)

And, this is where we (the body of Christ) come in; remember in St. John 20:22-23, when He told His disciples to first receive the Holy Ghost, and after that, in verse 23, Jesus said they could remit sin (or forgive sin). Though they were His disciples, they weren't God. Only God has the power to forgive sin, so what is happening here? God put Himself in man by filling him with the Spirit. That's why He said you can't do anything without Him.

Salvation through grace is the work of God, but God needs someone to work through. That's why the body of Christ is so important to God. We must receive the Holy Ghost as God has chosen to give it. How did God, the Holy Spirit, choose to give Himself to the church? We will answer that question in a later topic.

Have you ever asked the Lord, "Why would you have your apostles tarry at Jerusalem for the Holy Ghost, before they could baptize and fulfill the great commission?"

The apostles had to receive authority from heaven. The authority is the Holy Ghost. The Holy Ghost is Jesus. Jesus is the High Priest. The High Priest calls His own name over you, fulfilling the great commission. The name of Jesus is the blood that He uses. And you and I are the applicators (Hyssop) in His hand. So let God use you.

Please read this carefully. We are the generation that God has chosen to enter into the holiest of holies which is behind the veil. It's very important that we follow the pattern of the apostles. If we believe in Jesus through their word, then Jesus will manifest Himself in our congregations as never before that we might fulfill that greater work.

DO IT HIS WAY. AMEN.

Jesus said you must be born again. So how is a person born again of water and spirit according to the scriptures?

"Jesus answered and said unto him, verily, verily I say unto thee, except a man be born again, he cannot see the kingdom of God. Nicodemus saith unto him, how can a man be born when he is old? Can he enter the second time into his mother's womb, and be born? Jesus answered, Verily, verily, I say unto thee, except a man be born of water and of the Spirit, he cannot enter into the kingdom of God. That which is born of the flesh is flesh; and that which is born of the Spirit is spirit. Marvel not that I said unto thee, ye must be born again.

The wind bloweth where it listeth, and thou hearest the sound thereof, but canst not tell whence it cometh, and whither it goeth: so is everyone that is born of the Spirit" (*St. John 3:3-8).*

In order for us to enter the kingdom of God, we must turn to the man to whom God gave the keys to the Kingdom of Heaven. Now, according to scripture, in Matthew 16:13-20, God gave the keys of the kingdom of heaven to Simon Peter. On the day of Pentecost, those who were visiting Jerusalem, found in Acts 2:37, asked Simon Peter and the rest of the apostles what they must do. Peter replied, using the keys he received from God, and told them how to be born of water and Spirit.

"Then Peter said unto them, repent and be baptized every one of you in the name of Jesus Christ for the remission of sins, and ye shall receive the gift of the Holy Ghost" (*Acts 2:38). This is how you are born again according to the word of God.*

Peter didn't ask them to pray a sinner's prayer. Neither did he tell them that if they prayed a sinner's prayer, that they were automatically filled with the Holy Ghost and washed in Jesus' blood by faith.

The sinner's prayer in our generation has replaced God's great commission on most Christian Television Programs. In writing this book, there were many things considered. I could have been secretive as most ministers are in the public eye, not talking about certain topics and issues that are not popular in some church settings.

Ministers are often coached in what to say and what not to say, if they want to be accepted and successful. Yes, truly we all want to be accepted among our brethren. We want to be successful in ministry, but will God be pleased with us when it's all over? Micaiah took a stand for God by saying, "As the Lord liveth, what the Lord saith unto me, that will I speak." I Kings 22:14

We must not conceal the truth from the people of God just to prosper. I appreciate the fact that someone understood the word of God in how to prepare the heart for salvation, by allowing the believer to say a sinner's prayer. But, by no means should the sinner's prayer take the place of God's great commission. Will you allow the Holy Spirit to have His way in the midst of you, by doing what He has purposed to do from the foundation of the world? And because we love you so much, whether we are accepted or prosperous, it will not hinder us from exposing the truth. Every sinner's prayer must be fulfilled by God's great commission.

Please follow the Book of Acts, and do what the apostles did, if you want heaven to honor your salvation. Amen.

CHAPTER 3

What happens to a believer who is born of water, but not of spirit? What happens to a believer who is born of spirit, and not of water? Where are they found in scripture, or is it possible to have one without the other?

In the third chapter of St. John, Jesus was very explicit in telling Nicodemus that one must be born again of water and of spirit. In other words, Jesus was saying you couldn't have one without the other and enter into the kingdom of God. You need both water and Spirit births.

Are there examples in scripture where people were born of water and not of spirit? YES. In the book of Acts, chapter eight, Phillip, who was one of the first deacons, went down to Samaria and baptized believers in the name of Jesus. This was their water birth, but they hadn't received the Holy Ghost at that time. The scriptures don't say how long it was from the time of their birth (baptism in Jesus' name) until the moment Peter laid his hand on them, at which time they received the Holy Ghost. The scriptures tell us that they did not receive both at the same time.

Now the example of being born of Spirit before the water birth is found in Acts Chapter Ten. Peter is preaching Jesus unto Cornelius' household, and suddenly, the Holy Ghost falls on them and they began to speak in other tongues as they did on the day of Pentecost. That was their Spirit birth. So Peter said, "Can any man forbid water, that these should not be baptized, which have received the Holy Ghost as well as we?" (Acts 10:47).

Now, we understand God's requirement as to how we should be born of water and spirit. They are not automatically received when you pray a sinner's prayer. We must obey God's command.

I believe that those who are born of water but not of spirit are found in St. Matthew chapter twenty-five. If you notice, they were all virgins, five wise and five foolish. A virgin is an unmarried person. This person is pure and unblemished.

Paul said in Corinthians 11:2, "For I am jealous over you with godly jealousy: for I have espoused you to one husband, that I may present you as a chaste virgin to Christ." I believe that the blood of Jesus, which is applied by the Holy Ghost during water baptism, purifies a saint. The five foolish virgins represent those in the church who have been baptized with water in Jesus' name, but don't have oil in their lamps, which represents the Holy Ghost. The five wise virgins represent those saints who were not only washed in Jesus' blood, but had oil (Holy Ghost) in their lamps.

Now suppose a person received the Holy Ghost and then refused to be baptized in water in Jesus' name. Where are they in scripture?

I believe every believer must be washed in Jesus' blood. Every believer, after hearing the gospel, obtains faith, which is accounted to him as righteousness. That righteousness is a type of (spiritual) garment that must be washed in the blood of Jesus. That garment is made pure white and it covers our nakedness and shame, so that we might be clothed when He comes. Without the baptism is Jesus' name, God hasn't washed you in His blood and there are consequences found in Zephaniah 1:7-8.

The great day of the Lord is one where God will return for His people, but He will punish them in strange apparel.

"Hold thy peace at the presence of the Lord God: for the day of the Lord is at hand: for the Lord hath prepared a sacrifice, he hath bid His guests. And it shall come to pass in the day of the Lord's sacrifice, that I will punish the prince, and the king's children, and all such as are clothed with strange apparel" (*Zephaniah 1:7-8*).

Also, in the New Testament, you can find a guest not having a garment in St. Matthew 22:11. In this chapter, I ask the question, how were the guests without a wedding garment able to appear with the other guests in the presence of the king? And my other question is, where is this place? Is it in heaven or is it in the air?

Having the Holy Ghost is the only way that anybody, whether dead or alive, can be caught up to meet the Lord in air. If you notice, this is a type of wedding which is similar to the wedding of Christ which shall take place in the near future with His bride which is the church.

Now, there are some who disagree with this statement because they believe that nothing corrupt is getting up. But if you would examine scripture, Jesus said, "Let both grow together until the harvest: and in the time of harvest I will say to the reapers, Gather ye together first the tares, and bind them in bundles to burn them: but gather the wheat into my barn" (*St. Matthew 13:30, Also in St. Matthew 25:31-32*).

My reason for answering this question is to help my brothers who believe in the baptism of the Holy Ghost speaking in tongues, but refuse to call Jesus' name during water baptism. This is a great mistake. What man in his right mind would hinder Jesus from washing him in the blood? I want you to understand that Jesus is the High Priest dwelling in the man who is filled with the Holy Ghost speaking in other tongues as God gives him the utterance. Jesus uses the believer's body and voice to call His name over you which represents

His blood that is used to wash away your sins. This is how your raiment is made pure white. If the person baptizing with water leaves the name of Jesus out, the High Priest (who is Jesus Christ in you) will not have any blood for the atonement or removal of your sins. So I ask again what man in his right mind would turn Jesus away? Have you? This is the only way your name-brand garment can be made white. Amen.

Can I receive from God anything I need by faith without being saved?

"Now faith is the substance of things hoped for, the evidence of things not seen" (*Hebrews 11:1).*

Faith can be received by anyone and it does not matter if you are a saint or sinner. All you need is a pair of ears to hear or the ability to read lips or sign language. Why? Because "faith cometh by hearing, and hearing by the word of God" (*Romans 10:17).*

Faith is also given by God as a stimulus to help develop our mental, moral, and spiritual growth. Faith, in most cases, is used as a conveyance in scripture, which simply means, if you are going to receive anything from God you must have faith.

The people of faith in all denominations receive from God "all things that pertain unto life and godliness, through the knowledge of Him..." God also honors faith especially when it is exercised in His name. You don't have to be born again for God to honor your faith. For example, the centurion was not born again, but Jesus honored and acknowledged his faith by saying, "Verily I say unto you, I have not found so great faith, no, not in Israel" (Matthew 8:10). As a matter of fact, no one in scripture from Adam to the cross of Christ was born again, but they operated in faith and received from God that which they had need of. Please understand, that faith is not salvation.

In the book of Hebrews, chapter eleven, where it speaks of the heroes of faith, it says, "These all died in faith, not having received the promises, but having seen them afar off, and were persuaded of them, and embraced them, and confessed that they were strangers and pilgrims on the earth."

This is not written or revealed to discredit your faith in God, but that you might know that faith is not the blood of Jesus and it is not the Holy Spirit. Faith is only a channel by which you receive from God. "Without faith it is impossible to please Him" (*Hebrews 11:6a*).

Many people believe that when they receive a blessing of any type from God through their faith, they are saved. That's not true and it is a trick from the enemy. The woman who had the issue of blood was not saved, but she exercised faith by saying, "If I may but touch his garment, I shall be whole" (*Matthew 9:21*).

How do I know she wasn't saved? Jesus was not yet crucified. "Without the shedding of blood there's no remission. And where there is no remission there is no forgiveness. But thanks be to God who has given us salvation through the bloodshed of His son Jesus Christ."

I believe with all my heart that I should prosper and be in health even as my soul prosper. The prosperity message has hinder fellowship in the Body of Christ, Many Jesus name churches don't want faith teachers coming to their church preaching on money blessing (Name It and Claim It). There are thousands of small churches through out America, afraid to teach the saints how to receive from God material blessings through the confession of faith, Ultimately, not wanting to condemn themselves from past messages preached against Name It and Claim It.

It seems as if the pastors have taken a vow of poverty. And some of the saints are struggling to pay their bills working everyday, some are very sick in their bodies, yet giving God the praise for their suffering. But sometime we suffer because of our ignorance and a lack of knowledge.

Saints shouldn't have to leave one church to attend another that teaches faith. This is happening all over the country, in every city. I believe in holiness seven days a week, twenty-four hours a day, but I also believe that I should prosper in what ever I put my hands to do.

One church preaches Jesus Only and another preaches Faith Only. I believe God wants to bring the two together. Therefore we shouldn't throw anybody away. We ought to love one another and fellowship.

The Lord said, "is there any thing too hard for me?" Or is it the hardness of your heart?

Please don't misunderstand what we are saying, because I love all the people of God that walk by faith. Everyone needs faith to please God. As a matter of fact, you cannot receive anything from the Lord without faith. We must all exercise our faith through confession in prayer and in our everyday conversations. I am a student of Faith.

For the last seventeen years, my wife, children, and I have never lived in one place longer than four years. When God said move and go to the place He named, we packed up our belongings and left. Sometimes, we had to sell what we had. And whatever we had left, we took with us. One time, we only had a hundred and fifty dollars to travel over eight hundred miles with three children. Twenty years of traveling the highway, we never had a problem. Wherever we went, we never had jobs set up before we got there. We believed God and He always provided. This has happened to us many times, but God has never failed us. We were called the new saints. And believe me, it takes faith to dwell in a place where you are new, and having to prove your love for God with people that you are unfamiliar with. Therefore, I thank God for the faith He has given us to accomplish the things we have accomplished.

As a matter of fact, all the revelations read in this book came from my confession of faith. And my favorite scripture in prayer is Ephesians 1:17-19 which says, "That the God of our Lord Jesus Christ, the Father of glory, may give unto you (me) the spirit of wisdom and revelation in the knowledge of Him: The eyes of your (my) understanding being enlightened; that ye (I) may know what is the hope of His calling, and what the riches of the glory of His inheritance in the saints, And what is the exceeding greatness of His power toward us who believe, according to the working of His mighty power......"

So can I receive from God anything I have need of by faith without being saved? Yes.

CHAPTER 4

Who Is the Holy Ghost? Is He Jesus or is He God? Maybe the third person of Trinity? What does scripture say?

Remember how you could go to your daddy and ask him anything that was on your mind? Well, the Father is like that with us and He made it plain when He said, "And what agreement hath the temple of God with idols? For ye are the temple of the living God; as God hath said, I will dwell in them, and walk in them; and I will be their God, and they shall be my people. Wherefore come out from among them, and be ye separate, saith the Lord, and touch not the unclean thing; and I will receive you, and will be a Father unto you, and ye shall be my sons and daughters," saith the Lord Almighty (*II Corinthians 6:6-18*).

He wants us to know as much as we can receive about Him, but we must develop a relationship with Him, that we might know who we are in Him, and what we are to Him. Then we must accept what He says we are to Him. There's nothing He loves more than for us to be as little children seeking the kingdom of God. For I am as a man before the Lord, knowing nothing but Jesus Christ and Him crucified. God will honor your word of faith if you seek His face in sincerity.

I trust that this will help you in your understanding of who the Holy Spirit is. In the book of Acts, chapter one verse eight, Jesus made it clear by saying, "But ye shall receive power, after that the Holy Ghost is come upon you: and ye shall be witness unto me both in Jerusalem, and in all Judea, and in Samaria, and unto the uttermost part of the earth." If you notice as you read this scripture in the spirit, Jesus tells you, that you will be a witness unto Him (meaning Himself) after you receive the spirit.

He is telling us that He is the power, which has come, as the Holy Ghost to dwell in whoever will receive Him. And know also this, the Holy Ghost is the same as the Holy Spirit. Once God has empowered you with Himself, you will experience the angels ascending and descending upon you because of the presence of God in you. Then you will see His miracles manifested as the word of God says, "And they went forth, and preached everywhere, the Lord working with them, and confirming the word with signs following." Amen. (St. Mark 16:20)

This won't cost you anything, if you would look at the previous verse (19) it says, "So then after the Lord had spoken unto them, He was received up into heaven, and sat on the right hand of God." So if Jesus is in heaven sitting at the right hand of God, that means you are in heavenly places in Christ, according to Ephesians 1:3. Why? Because you are in Christ and Christ is in you.

The phrase "the Third Person of the Trinity" is manmade. It is not found in scripture. God revealed or manifested Himself as the Father of creation, the Son in redemption, and as the Holy Spirit in the dispensation of Grace. The scripture doesn't refer to God as a person, but as the creator.

As I have said in previous answers, God is a Spirit. Christ is the flesh of God. II *Corinthians 5:19, I Timothy 3:16*

God is the Father of Christ. "For this cause I bow my knees unto the Father of Christ, of whom the whole family in heaven and earth is named, that He would grant you, according to the riches of His glory, to be strengthened with might by His spirit in the inner man; that Christ may dwell in your hearts by faith; that ye, being rooted and grounded in love, may be able to comprehend with all saints what is the breadth, and length, and depth, and height; and to know the love of Christ which passeth knowledge, that ye might be filled with all the fullness of God" *(Ephesians 3:14-19).*

I pray that this answer has been a blessing to you and your family. Amen.

The Bible says we will wear white robes in heaven (Revelations 3:4-5, 18; 4:4; 6:11; 7:13-14; 16:15; 19:8).

Are we wearing them NOW while we're upon the face of the earth or will we receive these garments after the rapture takes place?

There's a great deliverance about to occur in America and the world abroad. I was asked the question once, what does the gospel mean to you? My response was, "The gospel is the power of God unto salvation to everyone that believeth; to the Jew first, and also to the Greek" (*Romans 1:16).*

I see the gospel as God's way of clothing us spiritually. I also see the fulfillment of the gospel and the blood of Jesus in the Great Commission.

When a person hears the gospel, faith enters in his or her heart because they believe. The faith they received by hearing the gospel is accounted to them as righteousness (*Galatians 3:6).*

Righteousness is your spiritual robe (or fine linen) that you have on this very moment if you believe in the gospel. Then righteousness must be fulfilled (or completed) through the baptism in water as Jesus said to John in Matthew 3:15. "And Jesus answering said unto him, suffer it to be so now: for thus it becometh us to fulfill all Righteousness. Then he suffered him."

This righteousness is God's way of clothing us so that our nakedness does not appear (*Revelations 3:18).*

Revelations 19:18 tells us that this righteousness is fine linen clean and white. This fine linen is the same as the robe in Revelations 7:14. There's only one thing throughout the history of man that can make us clean and white and that is the blood of Jesus.

You receive the robe or fine linen while you are upon the earth. Why am I so sure? Because Jesus' blood was shed in the earth on Calvary's cross. The scriptures only support us receiving the blood of Jesus while we are on the face of the earth. Once you die, it is too late. "And as it is appointed unto men once to die, but after this the judgment" (Hebrews 9:27).

That's why the scripture says, "Wherefore as the Holy Ghost saith, today if ye will hear His voice, harden not your hearts..." *(Hebrews 3:7b, 8a).*

My friend, please take heed to what God is saying to you, because you don't know what day will be your last day on earth.

How does a believer, once receiving his garment, keep it clean? If you have been washed in the blood of Jesus and commit a sin, the word of God says, "If we confess our sins, He is faithful and just to forgive us our sins, and to cleanse us from all unrighteousness, if we say that we have not sinned, we make Him a liar, and his word is not in us" (*I John 1:9,10).*

Also, it is very important to attend Bible study. Why? Because throughout your everyday cares, you sin against God unaware and when you are listening to the word of God, there's a searching taking place within your heart and it shows you your faults. When you are saved, the word doesn't come to condemn you (as to destroy), but to keep you clean. Notice what it says, "...that He might Sanctify and cleanse it with the washing of water by the word, that he might present it himself a glorious church, not having spot, or wrinkle, or any such thing; but that it should be holy and without blemish" (*Ephesians 5:26,27*).

Having God's words in your mouth is like living water flowing in the ears of the hearers. And it cleanses the soul.

Please understand this, even though you are a child of God, and an heir of God and joint heir with Christ, there must be a continuous cleansing in reference to your robe.

Your pastor or minister is a believer and should be filled with the word of God. The word says, "He that believeth on me, as the scripture hath said, out of his belly shall flow rivers of living water" (*John 7:38*).

That water is the word of God that cleanses you whether you are teaching the word or being taught the word. This is God's way of keeping your garments clean, so that when He comes you will be ready.

This revelation has been given to us so that we might prepare for the coming of the Lord. God has shown me that there are millions in the world possessing garments, but they are not yet clean for a lack of knowledge.

Now, my brothers and sisters, seeing that God has revealed unto you this revelation, I say unto you as Joseph said unto Pharaoh, "Look out a man discreet and wise." He must also be authorized by God to cleanse your garments. This is a crucial time in the history of the church.

Please do not let tradition keep you from making this important transition. Remember the words of the Lord.

"Behold, I come as a thief. Blessed is he that watcheth, and keepeth his garments, lest he walk naked, and they see his shame. Wherefore, beloved, seeing that ye look for such things, be diligent that ye may be found of him in peace, without spot, and blameless" (*Revelations 16:15; II Peter 3:14).*

CHAPTER 5

What is God looking for on Earth before He returns; is it just faith?

There are many things that God is looking for on earth before He returns for the church. We know that we are to have faith in God. And we should also have, "the fruit of the spirit which is love, joy, peace, longsuffering, gentleness, goodness, faith, meekness, temperance.... and they that are Christ's have crucified the flesh with the affections and lusts" (*Galatians 5:22-24).*

But inclusive of the fruit of the Spirit, there's something specifically that God is looking for according to scripture.

In the Second Coming of the Lord, God will appear unto them that are looking for Him (*Hebrews 9:28).*

The Lord has a watchful eye that runs to and fro throughout the earth. The return of the Lord will be like unto the days of Noah. So, therefore, I believe that God has placed on my heart to answer this question using Noah's Ark as an example. Now you may ask yourself, how can Noah's Ark compare to what God is looking for on earth before His return? Take a moment and think about this scripture that says: "But as the days of No'e were, so shall also the coming of the Son of man be. For as in the days that were before the flood they were eating and drinking, marrying and giving in marriage, until the day that No'e entered into the ark, and knew not until the flood came, and took them all away; so shall two be in the field; the one shall be taken, and the other left" (*Matthew 24:37-40).*

Now, I know that there are many interpretations of Noah's preparation of the ark. So bear with me in my interpretation of its meaning. I believe that the ark is a type of Jesus Christ. The animals of all sort that filled the ark represent the people of all nations, kindred, and tongues.

The three floors, I believe, symbolize the three manifestations of God, as the Father, as the Son, and as the Holy Ghost. The one door represents Jesus as the door of the sheepfold, and the one window, which allowed light into the ark, "was the true Light, which lighteth every man that cometh into the world" *(St. John 1:9).*

God was watching Noah carry out His command. God was also waiting for the last animal to enter into the ark. So how can that compare unto the church and what God is looking for in the last days? No one can enter or be a part of the body of Christ except he or she is born again of water and spirit. There were many animals in the forest, but God only chose two of every sort and destroyed the rest. Are you one of the two? Simple. You must be born again. God has not chosen everyone, because the word says, "Many are called, but few chosen" (*Matthew 22:14*).

Yes, I believe that the person in this chapter may have prayed a sinner's prayer and received the Holy Spirit, but he hadn't received the blood of Jesus. Is that possible for a believer not to have the blood? Yes, read it for yourself. He didn't have a garment on and therefore, he was naked. So what was missing? The blood.

And that's what God is looking for before He returns. **God is looking for His blood upon all His chosen. They are the ones that made themselves ready in Revelations 19:7-9.**

In Exodus 12:13, God was looking for the blood. When you receive Jesus as your Savior and obey His command by being washed in His blood and filled with His Spirit, you enter into the ark of safety.

CHAPTER 6

Is there any place in scripture, which indicates that God requires you to speak in other tongues as evidence of you having the Holy Ghost?

From the time of Jesus' ascension to this very day, the question has been asked, "Does everyone speak in tongues when they receive the Holy Ghost?" The question is not a matter of everyone speaking in tongues, but does God require us to speak in tongues as evidence of His presence in us. Some who have never spoken in tongues may say that God doesn't require everyone to speak in tongues, because not everyone has the gift of tongues.

Then, on the other hand, those who have the Holy Ghost speaking in other tongues as the Lord gives them utterance say everyone should speak in tongues or you are not born of the spirit.

Let us keep in mind that no one has a private interpretation of scripture. We should be lead by the actions of God in the scripture. We should not allow the words of men to lead us wrong no matter what their reputation is. Sometimes, we allow phrases such as "the moment you believe you are sealed with the Holy Spirit of promise and there are no physical experiences taking place." This statement is taken from the book of Ephesians 1:13-14 which says, "In whom ye also trusted after that ye heard the word of truth, the gospel of your salvation: in whom also after that ye believed, ye were sealed with that Holy Spirit of promise, which is the earnest of our inheritance until the redemption of the purchased possession, unto the praise of His glory." If you would notice in scripture the Bible does not say the moment you believe you are sealed. But it does say after that ye believed, ye were sealed, which means that God fulfilled His promise in every believer's life.

If you say the moment a person prays a sinner's prayer, they are instantly sealed (stamped) with the Holy Spirit, you will hinder them from receiving God's primary source of power. If Peter, James, and John with the rest of the apostles were on the face of the earth today, what would they teach or ascribe in reference to one receiving the Holy Spirit? Only what they themselves had experienced.

The word says in Acts chapter eight, the people believed Philip's preaching and yet the Holy Ghost had not fallen upon any of them. So what physical evidence were they listening for? The utterance of the Holy

Spirit, which is speaking in other tongues. And also, if you notice, they were believers and they were not filled with the Holy Ghost the moment they believed. If you find one place in the word of God that contradicts what someone has said, then the statement is not true.

My brothers and sisters, we have the word of God as our confidence and proof that God has given us His Spirit speaking in other tongues as He gives us the utterance.

Many times, when we share our testimony about the Holy Ghost, people think you are trying to put them in hell if they haven't spoken in tongues, but that is quite the contrary, for our objective is to keep them out of hell and from being eternally separated from God.

Please understand that this is how you are known of God when He returns for His church (*Galatians 4:9).*

If you do not have the Spirit of the Lord, He will say unto you, "I never knew you: depart from me, ye that work iniquity" (*Matthew 7:23b).* This is also how God quickens or transforms you at his return for the church (Romans 8:11; I Corinthians 15:51-8).

We are required or commanded by God to be born again of water and spirit. And to be born of spirit is to receive the spirit the way God chose to give it. Now if God chose to give His Spirit to every son or daughter speaking in other tongues as He did on the day of Pentecost, who are we to change His choice of action and hinder the power of God in the lives of His people? *(Acts 2:1-5)*

Shouldn't you think He would require the same thing of you as He did for His disciples to enter His kingdom? God has no respect of person. What He did for them He will do for you, whether at the moment of belief or sometime later down the road, you will receive the Holy Ghost, and He will speak in tongues. Remember He told His disciples to tarry at Jerusalem until they were endued with power? They didn't know how God would manifest the power in them. They were simply being obedient to the Lord's command by waiting for the promise at Jerusalem.

When the promise came, they had nothing to do with the tongues by which they uttered. That was God's doing. It was a sign to them that they had received His promise. The people visiting on the day of Pentecost were in question about what they heard, so Peter stood up and said, "But this is that which was spoken by the prophet Joel; And it shall come to pass in the last days, saith God, I will pour out of my spirit upon all flesh: and your sons and your daughters shall prophesy, and your young men shall see visions, and your old men shall dream dreams: And on my servants and on my handmaidens I will pour out in those days of my spirit; and they shall prophesy: And I will show wonders in heaven above, and signs in the earth beneath; blood, and fire, and vapor of smoke: The sun shall be turned into darkness, and the moon into blood, before that great and notable day of the Lord come: And it shall come to pass, that whosoever shall call on the name of the Lord shall be saved" (*Acts 2:16-21*).

So ask yourself this question, does God require me to receive His Spirit speaking in other tongues as He gives me the utterance and as the evidence that I have the power of God living in me? Now, ask yourself this question also: How would they have known if they had the Holy Ghost without speaking in tongues? Your answer would be they wouldn't have known. The same principle applies to you. If you haven't spoken in tongues, you're not sure you have the Holy Ghost. So ask God to clarify Himself in you. Don't play Russian Roulette with your salvation.

Yes, God is requiring the same utterance from you because He is the Lord and He changeth not.

Now if some one should say, not everyone speaks in tongues because every saint is not given the gift of tongues. This is not true, but our commentary is not on the gift of tongues, which is the next level for the spiritually mature. Everyone receives the promise of the Spirit, which was heard for the first time on the day of Pentecost. And without that utterance you can never receive the gift of tongues. Do you want the Holy Ghost?

If you said yes, I want the Holy Ghost speaking in other tongues as the spirit gives me utterance. See instructions on page 40.

Amen.

Did anyone in the Bible pray a sinner's prayer for salvation? Why do we pray sinner's prayers?

What scriptures are used to justify believers praying a sinner's prayer?

The Philippian Jailor was told by Paul and Silas to "believe on the Lord Jesus Christ, and thou shalt be saved, and thy house" *(Acts 16:31).*

In Romans, "If thou shalt confess with thy mouth the Lord Jesus, and shalt believe in thine heart that God hath raised Him from the dead, thou shalt be saved" (Romans 10:9).

Also, in First John verse nine, "If we confess our sins, He is faithful and just to forgive us our sins, and to cleanse us from all unrighteousness."

Though these are used to vindicate reason for the uses of sinner's prayers, no one in scripture ever prayed a sinner's prayer for salvation. Praying a sinner's prayer prepares your heart or spirit to receive from God His promise of salvation. Therefore, you shouldn't stop at the sinner's prayer, but you must continue on and receive God's total plan of salvation. God will teach you and bring you to the place where His blood is applied to your soul and the infilling of the Holy Spirit which is your born-again experience.

THE WORD OF GOD DOES NOT CONTRADICT ITSELF!

Jesus said, "He that believeth and is baptized shall be saved; but he that believeth not shall be damned. And these signs shall follow them that believe; In my name shall they cast out devils; they shall speak with new tongues; they shall take up serpents; and if they drink any deadly thing, it shall not hurt them; they shall lay hands on the sick, and they shall recover" (*St. Mark 16:16-18*).

Now the preachers of world say you don't have to be baptized to be saved. Some say baptism is not that important. It is just an outward witness or vindication of one's belief. The thief on the cross is used to justify this statement, by saying the thief on the cross was not baptized, but yet he was promised by Jesus to be with Him in His Kingdom. Many preachers say you don't have to speak in tongues to have the Holy Spirit, because not everyone has the gift of tongues, referring to the twelfth and fourteenth chapters of Corinthians.

My brothers and sisters, my philosophy is this, follow Jesus. Do what *He* says. If Jesus says be baptized (which is to be baptized in water), you get baptized. So what if they talk about you, at least you were obedient to what the Lord said to do. What's more important, what people say about you or doing what the word says? Make sure that the person who baptizes you has the Holy Ghost speaking in other tongues himself. Why?

Because that man is born of the spirit and Jesus lives in him. And only Jesus can wash away your sins.

This is not written to condemn anyone, but telling partial truths cannot bring a spiritual awakening in America and the world abroad.

The devil is yawning and patting his mouth. Why? Because there is no power and blood in most of our churches.

But where there is blood (water baptism in Jesus' name), power (receiving the Holy Ghost), and confession of faith by which God has established for salvation and true deliverance. Read Acts 8:1-4 and you will see how the church was persecuted because of the truth. Has Satan changed from those days? Does America have spiritual power over the devil to stop him from persecuting the church? No, for the most part, even we who are born again cannot stop him from persecuting us, but God can. So why is Satan so quiet? I believe that over half of the world has not received the blood of Jesus nor has been born of the Spirit. Why should Satan persecute those whom he already has? And those in sheep's clothing work for him to hinder those who would tell the truth. How is that possible?

Whenever the baptism in Jesus' name is mentioned on any national television program, that ministry will be immediately ostracized, belittled, mocked, and condemned by the preachers of the world. When the altar call is made, they ask the people to say a sinner's prayer, something established by them. When the altar call was made on the Day of Pentecost, the preacher said, "Repent and be baptized every one of you in the name of Jesus Christ for the remission of sins, and ye shall receive the gift of the Holy Ghost" (*Acts 2:38*).

We all want a spiritual awakening in America. We have prayed and asked God to send a revival. If you are afraid to stand up for that which is right, then how can you call yourself Christ-like? To be like Christ is to walk in the spirit. Let's take America and the world for Christ.

You especially, that have reached national recognition, God has put you there so that you would, "Let this mind be in you, which was also in Christ Jesus: Who, being in the form of God, thought it not robbery to be equal with God: But made himself of no reputation, and took upon him the form of a servant, and was made in the likeness of men: And being found in fashion as a man, he humbled himself, and became obedient unto death, even the death of the cross" (*Philippians 2:5-8*).

How to Receive The Holy Ghost

First of all understand this, the Holy Ghost is the same as the Holy Spirit. There is no difference! "God is a Spirit: and they that worship Him must worship Him in spirit and in truth" (*John 4:24*).

If you have not received the Spirit of God, you cannot worship God in spirit. Therefore, everyone who calls upon the Lord is not a true worshipper, (not having the Spirit). So it is important to receive the Holy Spirit the way God chose to reveal or manifest Himself in us. *(See Acts 2:1-5.)*

But once you receive the Holy Ghost, you will have the power not only to worship, but you are an extension of God's authority on the earth. This book is written for those who have chosen to reject the manifestation of God in us through the evidence of speaking in tongues as He (God) gives the utterance. And to those who have not received the power of God, but have a great desire to submit to His perfect will in their lives; that God might walk in them as He walked in Christ.

God wants to control the part of your body that has the power of life and death. "Death and life are in the power of the tongue: and they that love it shall eat the fruit thereof" *(Proverbs 18:21).*

Which fruit do you desire to eat? The fruit of life or the fruit of death? The scripture says, "And they that love it shall eat the fruit thereof." In other words, you will eat of one or the other; there is no in between. When you receive the Holy Ghost, you will be led into all truth. This truth comes from the spoken word of God that proceeds out of your mouth being inspired by the Holy Ghost, thereby allowing you to receive the blessing of God in your life. Now, on the other hand, if you have not received the Holy Ghost, who are you led by?

Can a man receive the material things of this life without the Holy Ghost, sure, but they are temporal. "There is a way which seemeth right unto a man, but the end thereof are the ways of death" *(Proverbs 14:12).*

The apostle John said, "Even the spirit of truth whom the world cannot receive, because it seeth Him not, neither knoweth Him: but ye know Him; for He dwelleth with you, and shall be in you" *(John 14:17).*

Joel prophesied before Jesus was born saying, "And ye shall eat in plenty, and be satisfied, and praise the name of the Lord your God, that hath dealt wondrously, with you: and my people shall never be ashamed. And ye shall know that I am in the midst of Israel, and that I am the Lord your God, and none else: and my people shall never be ashamed. And it shall come to pass afterward, that I will pour out my spirit upon all flesh; and your sons and your daughters shall prophesy, your old men shall dream dreams, your young men shall see visions: And also upon the servants and upon the handmaids in those days will I pour out my spirit" *(Joel 2:26-29).*

Are you ready to receive to the Holy Ghost now?

First, hear the gospel. Then repent. You must understand that there are many ways to receive the Holy Ghost, but you must have faith.

You can receive the Holy Ghost by laying on of hands. *(See Acts 8:17.)*

You can receive the Holy Ghost before you are baptized in water in Jesus' name. *(See Acts 10:47.)*

You can receive the Holy Ghost after the water baptism in Jesus name. *(See Acts 19:6.)*

All God wants to know is do you want to receive His promise the way He chose to give it? If so, read *Acts 2:1-5.*

Next, ask God to fill you with His Spirit. *(See Luke 11:13.)*

Then you must believe by faith that you have received the Holy Ghost. You do not have to tarry for it because the spirit has already been poured out. Just open your heart and praise him for giving you His Spirit by saying Alleluia. This is the highest praise you can give God. *(See Revelation 19.)*

As you praise the Lord by saying Alleluia, God will manifest His presence within you by the evidence of speaking in other tongues. If perhaps you don't receive the manifestation of the Holy Ghost the first time, don't give up. Continue to praise Him in prayer every day until He manifests Himself in you as He did on the Day of Pentecost.

If this is any consolation to you, it took me three months to receive the Holy Ghost speaking in other tongues. And when I received it, I was in my bedroom.

So God can fill you anywhere, all you have to do is seek His face. Amen.

What is being said to hinder believers from receiving the Holy Ghost?

It is the word of God itself. Just as one can use the word of God to build faith to receive the Holy Ghost, the word of God can also be used to hinder your growth when it is taken out of context and misinterpreted.

For instance, some justify their lack of speaking in tongues by going to I Corinthians 13:8b, which says, "Whether there be tongues, they shall cease." But the question is, has God stopped pouring out His Holy Spirit? And has He changed his mind about the way He chose to manifest Himself in His people by giving them utterance in other tongues? No.

When God takes the church out of this realm, tongues will cease, and there will be no more outpouring of God's Spirit. Then tongues will cease. But the church is still here, and God is continuing to empower His body.

Then someone asked the question, "Do all speak with tongues?" (See I Corinthians 12:30b.) No, and if you notice the word "tongue" has an "s" at the end, which signifies different utterances and denotes the gift of tongues which everyone has not. But does everyone speak in tongues when they receive the Holy Ghost? Yes, absolutely, positively, and without a shadow of a doubt. Why am I so sure? Because Jesus said it to Nicodemus, "So is everyone that is born of the Spirit." In other words, they will make that sound. (See St. John 3:8.) And the fulfillment of St. John 3:8 is Acts 2:1-5 when the sound came from Heaven and filled the whole house.

Now the scripture that is used to hinder saints from speaking in tongues in the church is taken from I Corinthians 14:19 which says, "Yet in the church I had rather speak five words with my understanding, that by my voice I might teach others also, than ten thousand words in an unknown tongue."

Paul did not write this to keep saints from speaking in tongues in the church, but that they may learn not to teach in tongues. Some fellow got up and started teaching in other tongues. He thought that since he and the others whom he was teaching spoke in tongues that they should understand what he was saying since they had the same power.

Therefore, Paul explains to the saints that taught in tongues that no one would understand him except he have an interpreter; and that tongues was for a sign to the unbeliever.

So, before you can receive the Holy Ghost speaking in other tongues, you must first believe by faith that you have received the Holy Ghost in your heart before God will manifest His utterance in your mouth.

How to loose yourself from the hindrance of the past.

The way you can loose yourself from the hindrance of the past is by using the word of God. "The word is nigh thee, even in thy mouth, and in thy heart: that is, the word of faith, which we preach." The Bible says, "According to your faith be it unto you. And their eyes were opened."

You will be loosed from that which has hindered you by the confession of your mouth. As you pray, ask God for the Holy Ghost (See Luke 11:13) then say to the Lord, "I receive your Holy Spirit as you gave it on the day of Pentecost." Proceed by praising Him saying, "Alleluia, Alleluia, Alleluia"...until God changes Alleluia into a beautiful unknown language. And as you are saying Alleluia, God is destroying every hindrance in your life and setting you free.

Understanding God's forgiveness after being forgiven.

One day, at the end of twelve o'clock prayer, I was walking down the aisle in the church and was almost to the main lobby. Suddenly, a gentleman opened the front door and entered the church. We greeted one another and inquired with small talk about one another's background. Then I asked the young man which church he attended. I don't really remember the name of the church, but he did say he was born again. So I proceeded to ask him how he

was born again, and he said he asked Jesus to forgive him of his sins. He didn't go into details, so I took the liberty to explain to him what forgiveness was.

I always thought that if I sinned against God though I was baptized in Jesus name, I was obligated to ask God for forgiveness. But this young man explained something to me that made so much sense, and what he said was, "If Jesus died for your sins and washed them away as the Bible says, then why must you continue to ask Him to forgive you?" What you must understand is that Jesus shed His blood once for sin, and that one time took care of every sin that you would ever commit then after. It really took me some time to understand that, because whenever I sinned against God I thought I needed God to forgive me after I confessed. So this young man made me think by using the word of God. In order for God to forgive your sins, there must first be the shedding of blood as it is recorded in the word of God, "Saying, This is the blood of the testament which God hath enjoined unto you. Moreover, he sprinkled with blood both the tabernacle, and all the vessels of the ministry, and almost all things are by the law purged with blood; and without shedding of blood is no remission." And the word goes on to say, "For by one offering he hath perfected forever them that are sancified" (Hebrews 9:20-22; 10:14).

In Ephesians chapter one and verse seven, it says, "In whom we have redemption through his blood, the forgiveness of sins, according to the riches of his grace..." and if you would notice the scripture, you can't find anyone asking for forgiveness after they've been washed or baptized in Jesus name. Why? Because God has purposed to wash away the guilt of sin with His blood that is applied during water baptism. So if you continue to ask Jesus for forgiveness after He has washed you in his own blood according to Revelation 1:5b, you are asking Jesus to go back to Calvary's cross and shed His blood all over again. Really you are refusing to accept what God has done in the regeneration. We say we believe, but our actions and words say otherwise. We all know that Jesus is not going back to Calvary's cross to shed blood anymore.

An individual who is coming to Jesus for the first time asks God for forgiveness because he hasn't been washed in Jesus' blood. Naturally, he or she has a guilty conscience. But you who are born again have come to God and are washed in his blood where your conscience has been purged. I want you to understand that God's blood never loses its power to forgive and deliver you once it has been applied. And what God does the first time, He does it perfectly.

So what must we do when we sin against God after we have been washed in his blood? We must do as the word said: "If we confess our sins, he is faithful and just to forgive us our sins, and to cleanse us from all unrighteousness. If we say that we have not sinned, we make him a liar, and his word is not in us" 1 John 1:9, 10.

God is faithful without you having to ask Him to be faithful. He will be faithful to forgive.

God is good. Whenever someone does something for me, I thank them for what they have done out of a heart of gratitude. So if we can thank others for what they have done for us, how much more is the Lord worthy of thanksgiving. So whenever you sin against God, simply repent and confess your sins and thank him for his forgiveness. After you accept God's forgiveness, the windows of heaven shall open unto you. God will also bring you close to him that you might know his love for you. He will also give you divine revelation of his word like you have never known before. I am truly grateful to the Lord for the manifestation of his hand in my life in raising the dead and opening blinded eyes in Montgomery, Alabama. In Champaign, Illinois, He healed the sick and caused the lame to walk. To God be the glory for all that He has done. Amen.

CHAPTER 7

Nakedness

"And Adam said, 'This is now bone of my bones, and flesh of my flesh: she shall be called Woman, because she was taken out of Man.' Therefore shall a man leave his father and his mother, and shall cleave unto his wife: and they shall be one flesh. And they were both naked, the man and his wife, and were not ashamed" (*Genesis 2:23-25*).

"Now the serpent was more subtle than any beast of the field which the Lord God had made. And he said unto the woman, yes, hath God said, ye shall not eat of every tree of the garden?"

Notice the Devil knew what God said to Adam before he approached Eve. Then he asked her a question to ignite her curiosity by saying, "Hath God said, ye shall not eat of every tree of the garden?"

There are times in our lives when Satan deceives us by not telling us the entire story. In the next few verses, Eve will tell the serpent what God said and then the serpent contradicted the commandment of God by telling her a part of the truth.

"And the woman said unto the serpent, We may eat of the fruit of the trees of the garden: But of the fruit of the tree which is in the midst of the garden, God hath said, Ye shall not eat of it, neither shall ye touch it, lest ye die. And the serpent said unto the woman, Ye shall not surely die: For God doth know that in the day ye eat thereof, then your eyes shall be opened, and ye shall be as gods, knowing good and evil" (V2-5).

What did the serpent deliberately withhold from Eve though he knew it? It withheld the fact that she was naked. Why? Because Satan wants you to be ashamed of the workings of God in your life and cause you to walk in the flesh. When God calls us out of darkness and washes away our sins, sometimes we stumble and fall back into sin, then we are ashamed of what we have done and stop coming to church so we don't have to face the saints. Satan can be very persuasive. Notice in the very next verse, Eve yields to the desires of her flesh.

"And when the woman saw that the tree was good for food (lust of the flesh), and that it was pleasant to the eyes (lust of the eye), and a tree to be desired to make one wise (the pride of life), she took of the fruit thereof, and did eat, and gave also unto her husband with her; and he did eat" (V6).

What holds people in bondage is the part truth spoken by Satan that comes to pass. Everything the Devil tells you is not a lie.

"And the eyes of them both were opened, and they knew that they were naked; and they sewed fig leaves together, and made themselves aprons" (V7).

The Lord is mindful of every condition and circumstance that arises in our lives. Adam and Eve heard the voice of God walking in the garden and hid themselves. So God wanted to know why and Adam said, "I was naked." Even though God issued them punishments for their disobedience, "The Lord God made coats of skins, and clothed them."

God clothed Adam and Eve to cover their shame. God has made provisions for you and I; just follow the outline.

How to purchase Name Brand (white raiment) for Heaven

In order for God to cover your nakedness, you must receive His righteousness. I have prepared an outline that will help you understand the gospel so that you might cover your nakedness.

First the gospel is preached, "So then faith cometh by hearing and hearing by the word of God" (*Romans 10:17*).

After hearing the word, you repent and then conversion will take place in your heart. This conversion or belief is called faith.

Faith

"Now faith is the substance of things hoped for, the evidence of things not seen" (*Hebrews 11:1*).

"And the scripture was fulfilled which saith, Abraham believed God, and it was imputed unto him for righteousness: and he was called the Friend of God" *(James 2:23)*.

After you receive faith, which is accounted unto you as righteousness, this righteousness is your wedding garment that you will need when you are raptured. Without this garment, you cannot participate in the marriage of the Lamb (St. Matthew 22:11-12).

Righteousness is given to you after you believe the gospel.

"But to him that worketh not, but believeth on him that justifieth the ungodly, his faith is counted for righteousness" (Romans 4:5).

"And to her (The Church) was granted that she should be arrayed in fine linen, clean and white: for the fine linen is the righteousness of saints" (*Revelation 19:8*).

The righteousness must be fulfilled by being baptized in water. Baptism in water under the law was unto repentance, which was by John the Baptist. Baptism under grace is the removing of sins by the Lord Jesus Christ. And through this process, your wedding garment is cleansed and made white by the blood of the Lamb (*Revelation 7:14*).

Righteousness is fulfilled in water baptism.

"But John forbade him, saying, I have need to be baptized of thee, and comest thou to me? And Jesus answering said unto him, suffer it to be so now: for thus it becometh us to **fulfill all righteousness**. Then he suffered him" (*Matthew 3:14, 15*).

"Go ye therefore, and teach all nations, baptizing them in the name of the Father, and of the Son, and of the Holy Ghost: Teaching them to **observe all things whatsoever I have commanded you**: and, lo, I am with you always, even unto the end of the world. Amen. (*Matthew 28:19, 20*).

So how is the Baptism performed?

Baptism

"Now when they heard this, they were pricked in their hearts, and said unto Peter and to the rest of the apostles, Men and brethren, what shall we do? Then Peter said unto them, repent, and be baptized every one of you in the name of Jesus Christ for the remission of sins, and ye shall receive the gift of the Holy Ghost" *(Acts 2:37, 38).*

Now this scripture comes to mind.

"Therefore leaving the principles of the doctrine of Christ, let us go unto perfection: not laying again the foundation if repentance from dead works, and of faith toward God, of the doctrine of baptisms, and of laying on of hands, and of resurrection of the dead, and of eternal judgment" *(Hebrews 6:1, 2).*

How can a man leave something he has never embraced? God gave us a Great Commission and many of the preachers today have nullified it making the Lord's command of no effect by saying you don't have to be baptized to be saved.

And the scriptures most preachers use are Romans 10:9 and Ephesians 2:8. Though you have faith, faith must be perfected by doing what God said to do.

In Acts 2:37, they asked the question, "What shall we do?" **Notice the word "do" in the scriptures.**

In Acts 9:6, Paul "...trembling and astonished said, Lord what wilt thou have me to do? And the Lord said unto him, Arise, and go in the city, and it shall be told thee what thou must do."

In Acts 10:6, the angel from heaven told Cornelius where to find Simon, "...whose surname is Peter: He lodgeth with one Simon a tanner, whose house is by the sea side: he shall tell thee what thou oughtest to do."

And last but not least, the Philippian prison keeper in Acts 16:30 who feared and would have taken his life said, "Sirs, what must I do to be saved?"

Abraham was obedient to God's command by doing what God told him to do. "And by works was faith made perfect?" (*James 2:22*)

God has perfected our faith through His blood and water. Amen.

"I counsel thee to buy of me gold tried in the fire, that thou mayest be rich; and white raiment, that thou mayest be clothed and that the shame of thy nakedness do not appear; and anoint thine eyes with eyesalve, that thou mayest see" (Revelation 3:18).

Have you purchased your heavenly garments from Jesus yet? Just do it!

Write to Pastor Johnny Ray Franklin Sr. at:
White Raiment Ministries
P.O. Box 2600
Laurel, MD 20709

Printed in the United States
69481LVS00001B/160-177